AF604911

HEY YOU! KEEP GOING

art by shuturp

INTRO

Hi! Welcome! Glad you're here. Are you comfy? My name's Ellie and this is a book of all my favourite drawings just for you. Take your time OR read it like i would, <u>really</u> fast. I'm so happy to share this little slice of my ADHD brain with you. How i see the world, big feelings and tips on how to get through it all. Thank you!

CONTENTS

FRIENDSHIP

CHEER THE FUCK UP
K

you look
tired

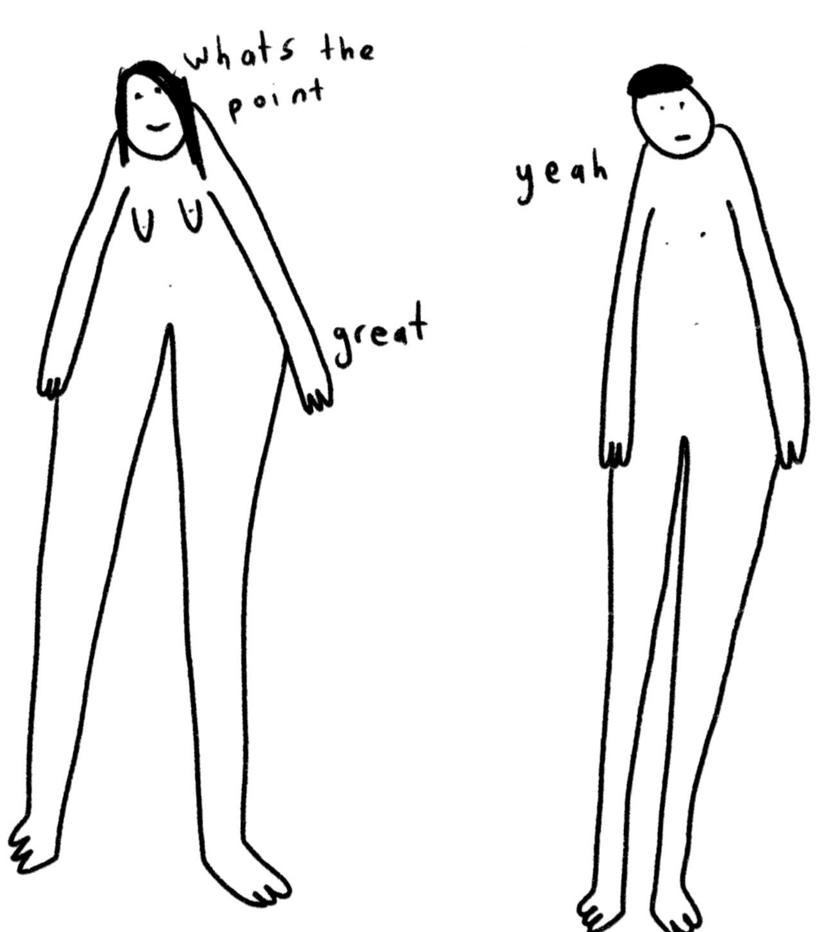
whats the point
great
yeah

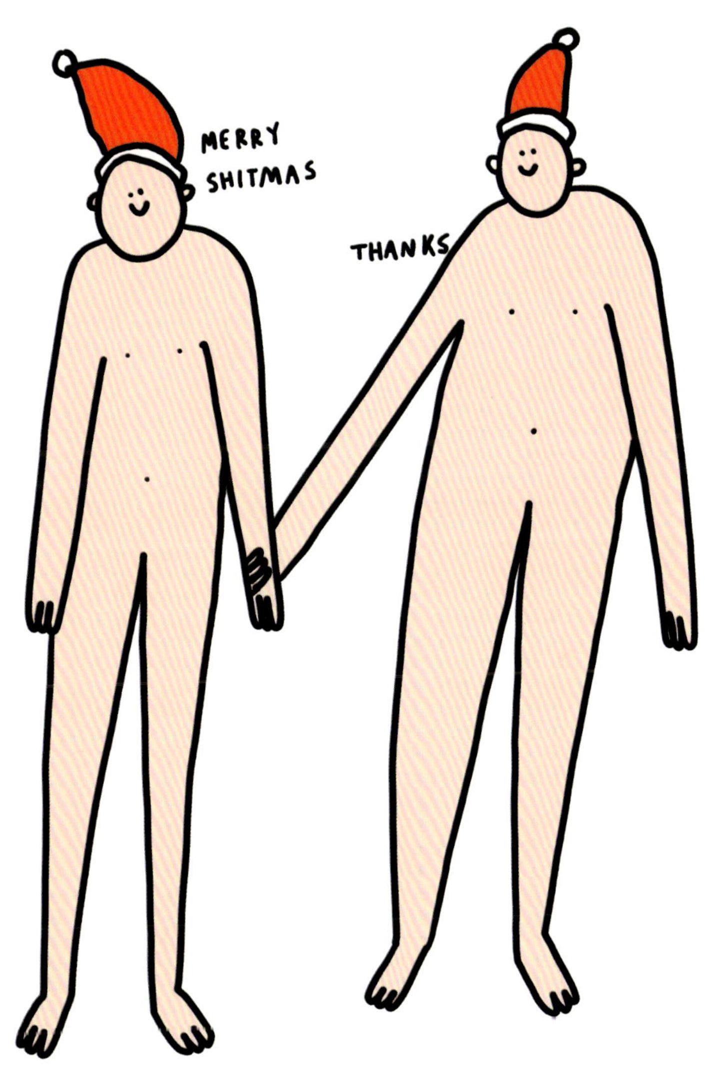
MERRY SHITMAS
THANKS

HOW'S LIFE
MATE
YES

to the
kebab shop
meow

TELL YOUR FRIENDS HOW YOU REALLY FEEL

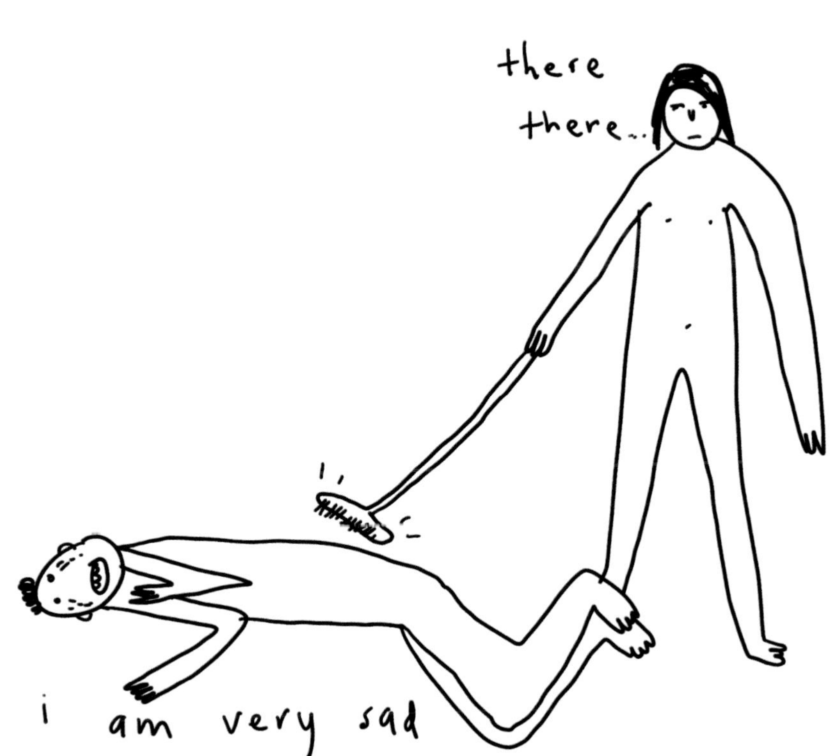
there
there...
i am very sad

LIFE IS TOO SHORT TO GIVE A SHIT

You look really tired helen
what!? I had absolutely no idea thanks so much for letting me know you are truly a star.

would you
like
to be
my
friend

what's your star sign
no thanks
im guessing Libra
please release me from this hell

THROW ALL
YOUR SHIT
FRIENDS IN THE
BIN

bye

PROTECT YOUR FRIEND FROM THIS TERRIBLE WORLD BY COVERING THEIR EYES

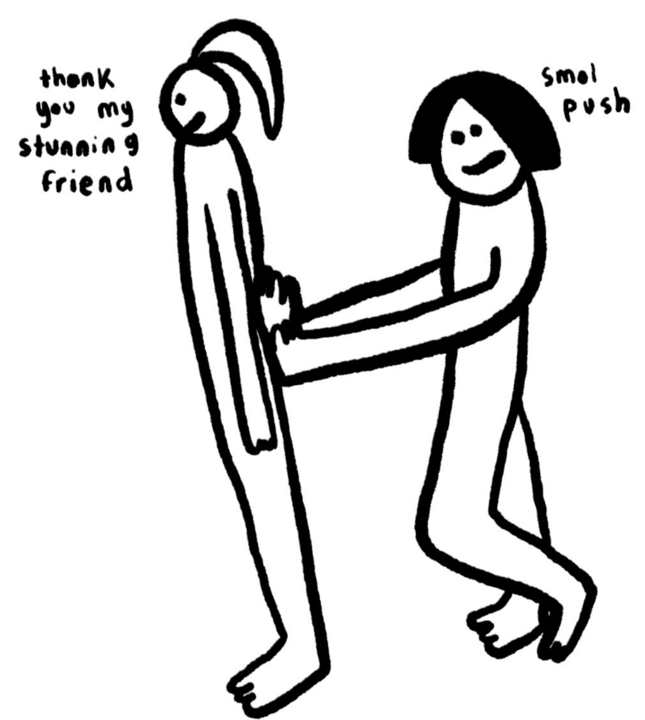

SOMETIMES YOU JUST NEED A SMALL PUSH

a fat
slow dog.

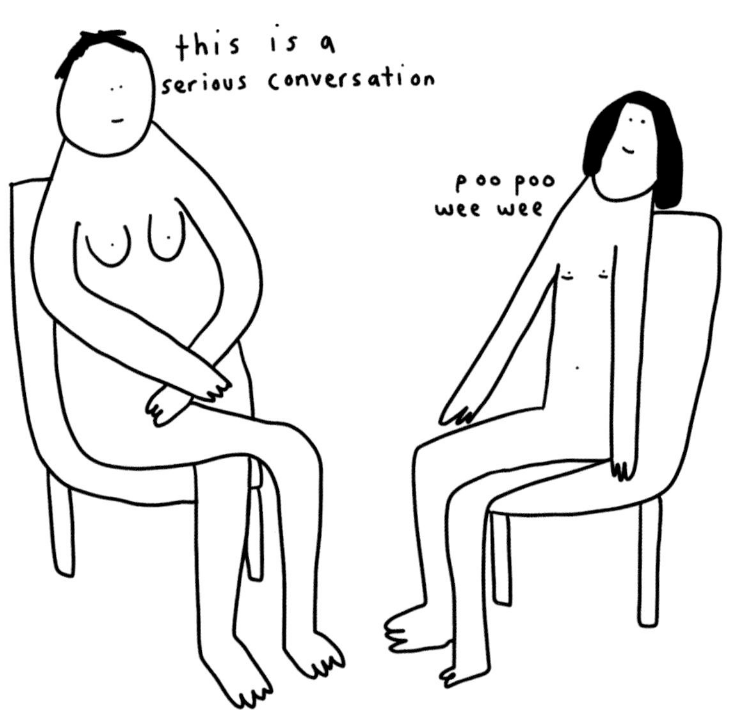
this is a serious conversation
poo poo wee wee

I WOULD
RATHER BE
ALONE THAN
IN BAD
COMPANY

LOVE

you dont need to
go looking for
love. its already
here

LOVE IS LIKE

GARLIC BREAD

AND IM SO

HUNGRY

here we have a
love heart with
some hair

can you
airdrop me
some love

HA omg no
im fine honestly

love is like a
warm blanket on a
rainy day. it's
also like riding a
horse that is
actually a dinosaur
with heaps of teeth

i got u
this leaf
that i found
on the
ground
omg how
thoughtful
i love
leaves

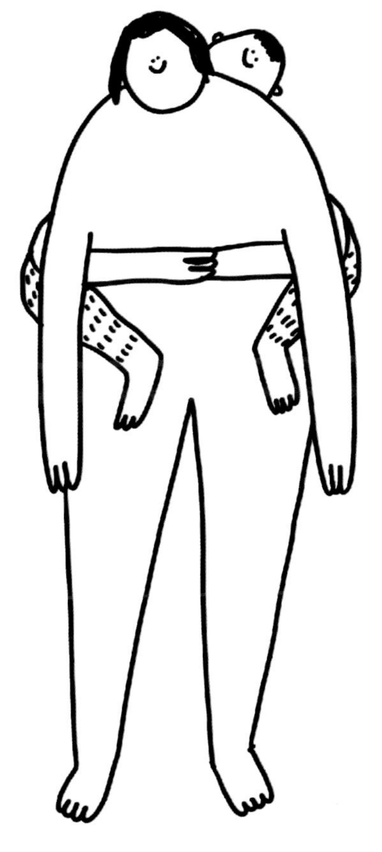

HUMAN BACKPACK

WE LOVE OUR BREAD
WE LOVE OUR BUTTER
BUT MOST OF ALL
WE HATE EACH OTHER
AND JUST LOVE THE

DOG

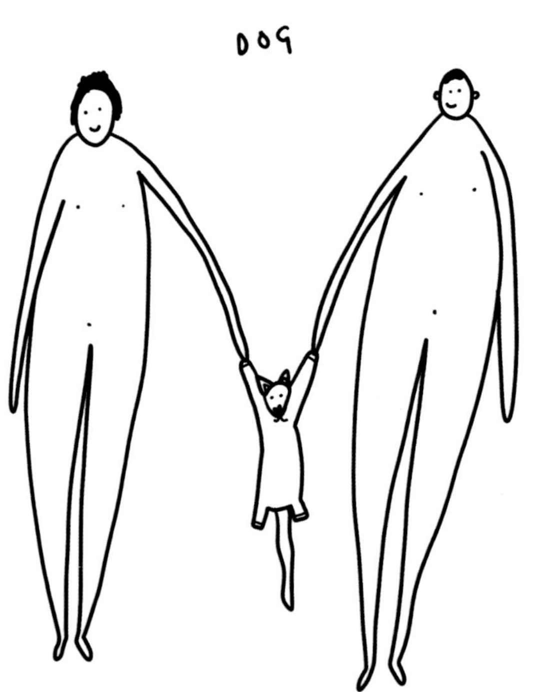

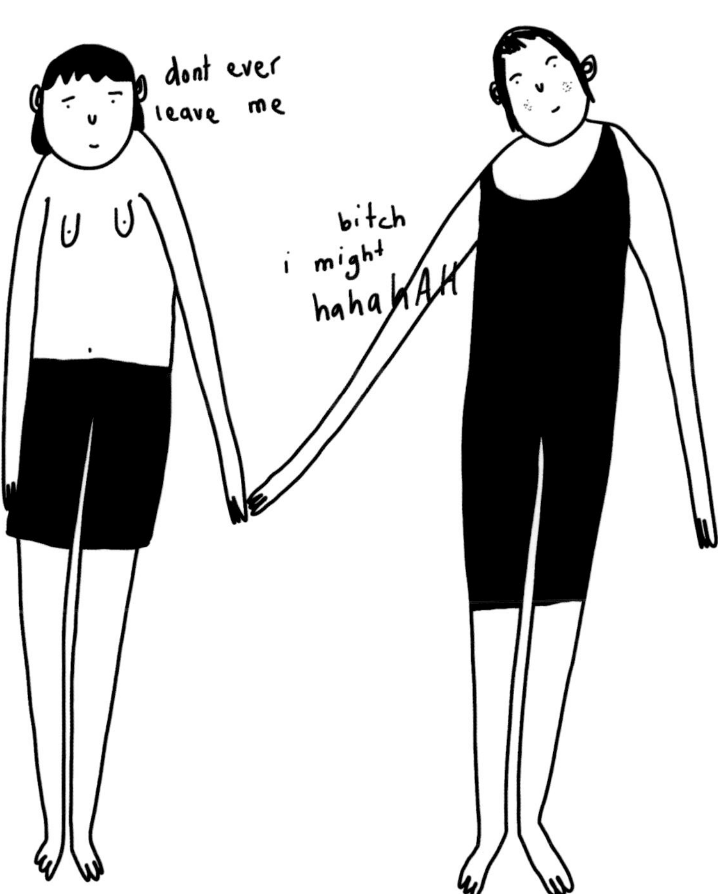
dont ever
leave me
bitch
i might
hahahAH

THROUGH IT ALL

FIRST DATE

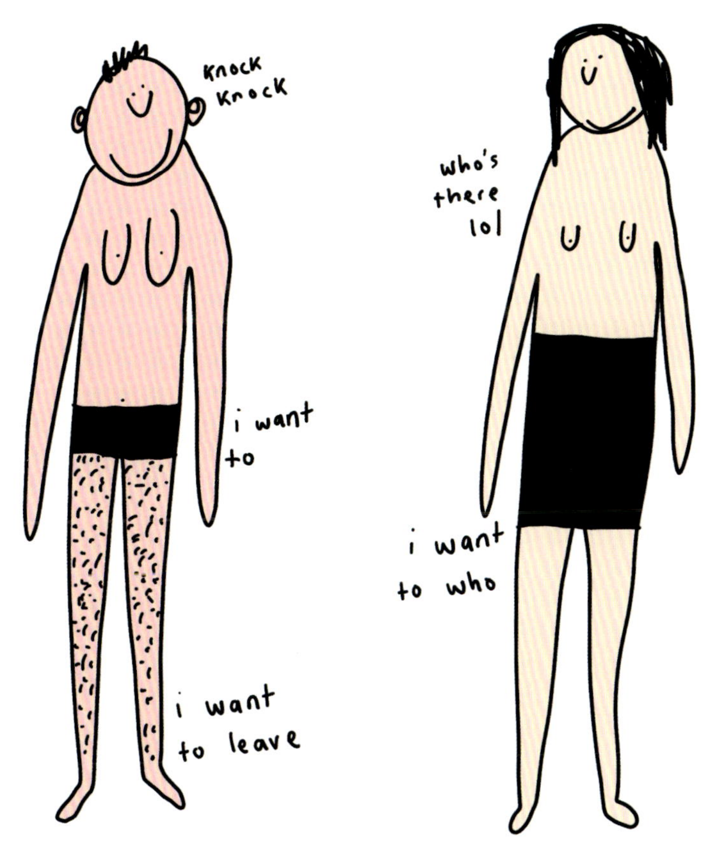
knock knock
who's there lol
i want to
i want to who
i want to leave

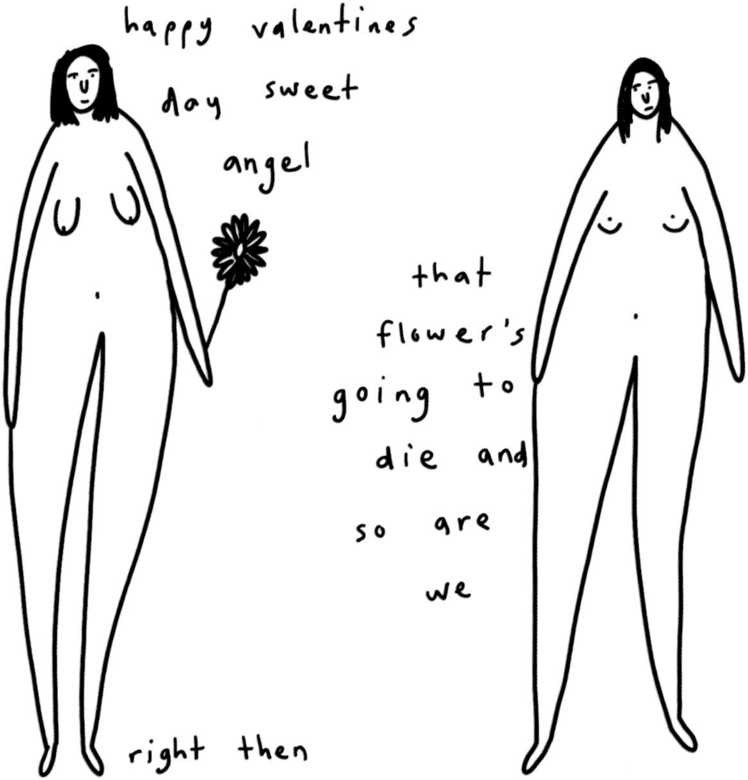

happy valentines
day sweet
angel

that
flower's
going to
die and
so are
we

right then

i got
u sum
flowers
ok but
im a
dog

my love language
is affection
what's yours
um mine is
probably don't
come anywhere
near me
unless I
say so

i need
to go to
work
quit

liv
larf
luv

i will
love u
until we're
fat and
old
and then
what

I BE LOVIN
BANANAS

CONFESS YOUR LOVE!

hug

THANK YOU FROM THE
BOTTOM OF MY HEART

anyways here is a
song i wrote about
how my heart got
ripped out of my
chest and run
over by a bus
full of raccoons

if i didn't
have this dog
i would
simply never
leave the
house

NEURODIVERSITY

OH DEARY ME
I THINK A MENTAL
BREAKDOWN IS
ON THE HORIZON

THIS BAD
FEELING WILL
PASS LIKE
THE CLOUDS IN
THE SKY

CAN'T DECIDE

WHAT NO
IM FINE
THANK YOU

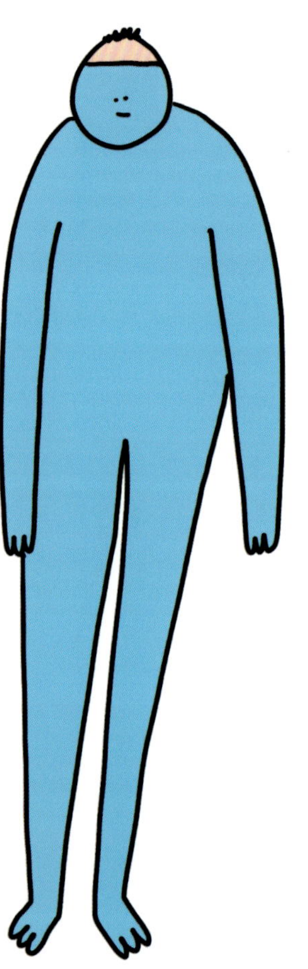

WORRY

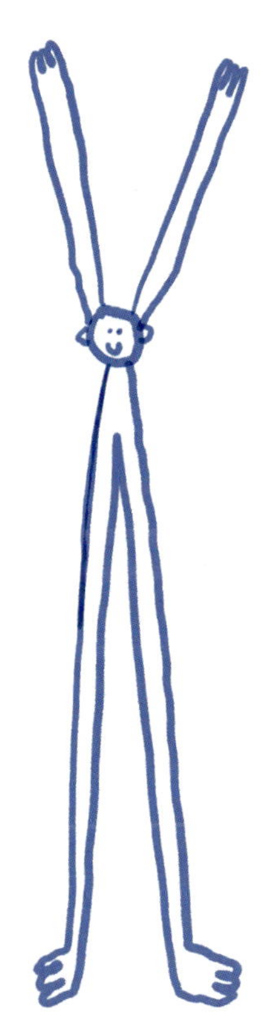

not really sure
but excited nevertheless

things
to do
this
is fine
me

TRYING
MY
BEST

MY
HEAD IS
TOTALLY
FULL OF
SHIT

I'M A FRUIT CAKE

NOBODY LIKES ME

good morning
to everyone
except the
people that chew
really loudly.

do you think
you could
stop following
me for like
one minute

no sorry
hun
ANXIETY

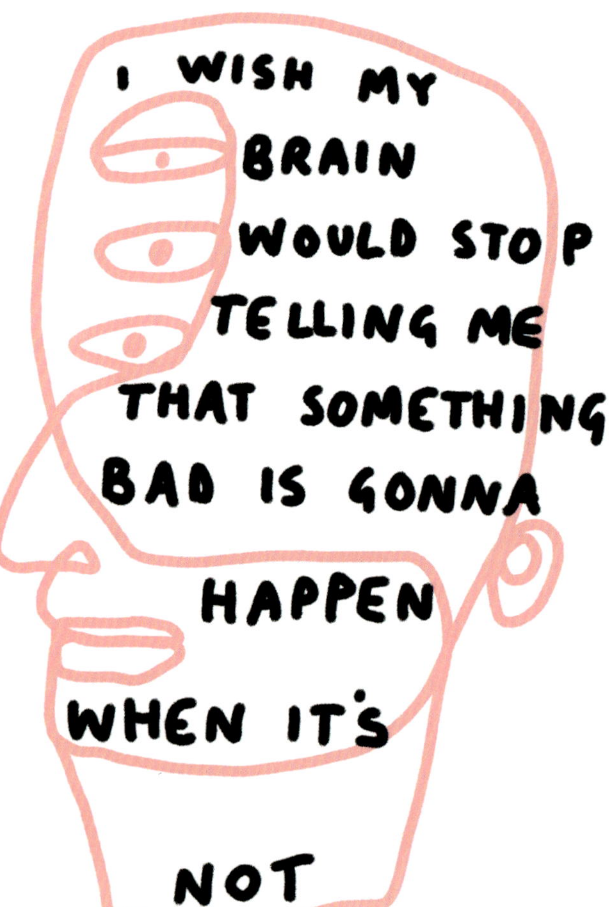
I WISH MY
BRAIN
WOULD STOP
TELLING ME
THAT SOMETHING
BAD IS GONNA
HAPPEN
WHEN IT'S
NOT

sweep it under the rug, babe

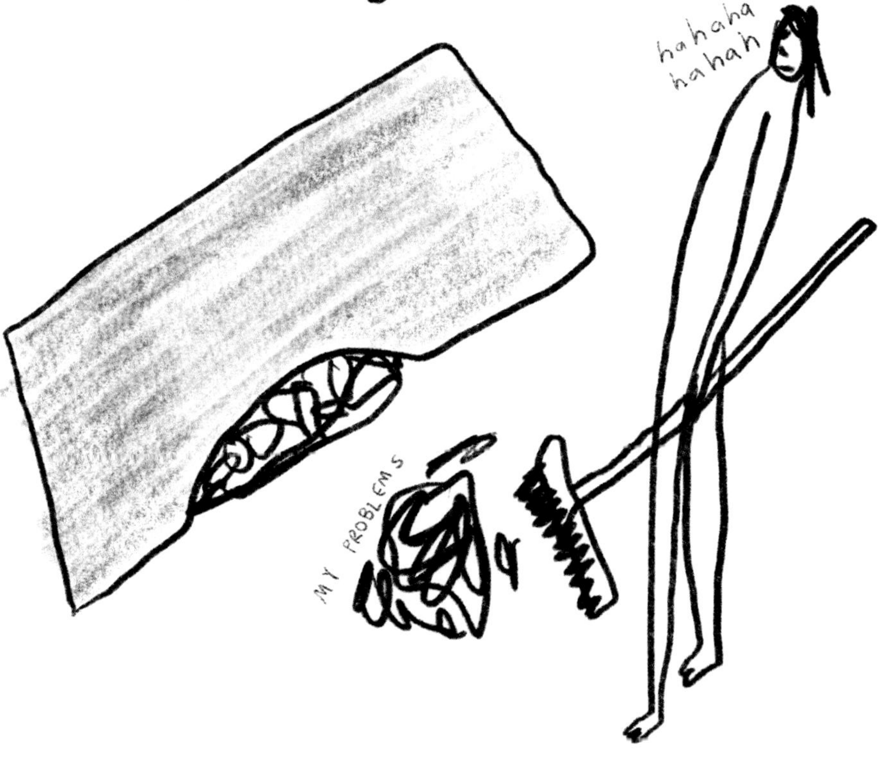

hahaha hahah

MY PROBLEMS

JUST GIVE ME
A MOMENT PLEASE
shuturp

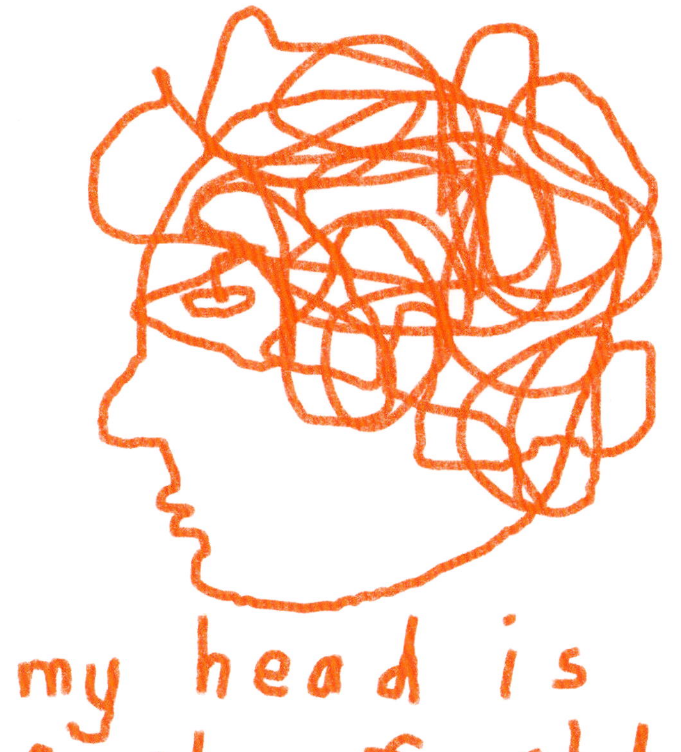

my head is
full of old
spaghetti

WHAT THE HECK

LIFE IS
TIRING

Sometimes i'm

happy sometimes

i'm sad. i'm a

bit like my mum

and a bit like

my dad.

depression

monster

sometimes
i think
so
deeply
that it
hurts
but
only sometimes

annoyed

but alive

A D H D

sitting down is
boring i would much
rather stand up

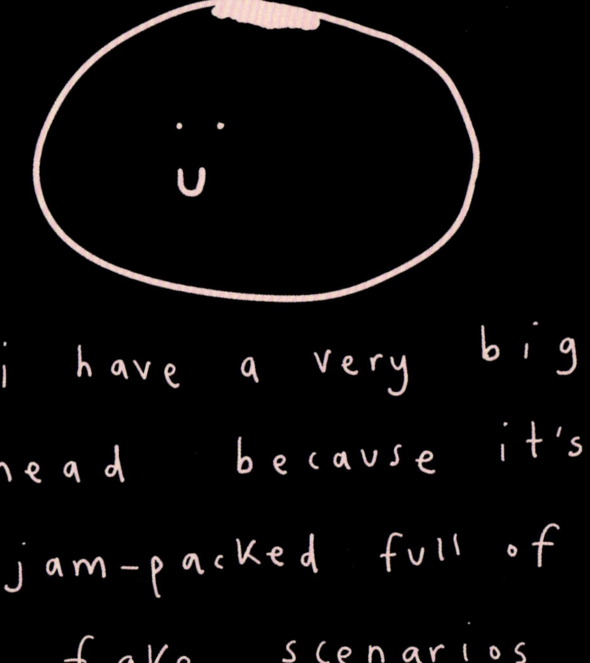
i have a very big head because it's jam-packed full of fake scenarios

i'm really
good at starting
stuff but
very bad at
finishi
n
g

RAAHHH I AM A BIG
SAD PERSON

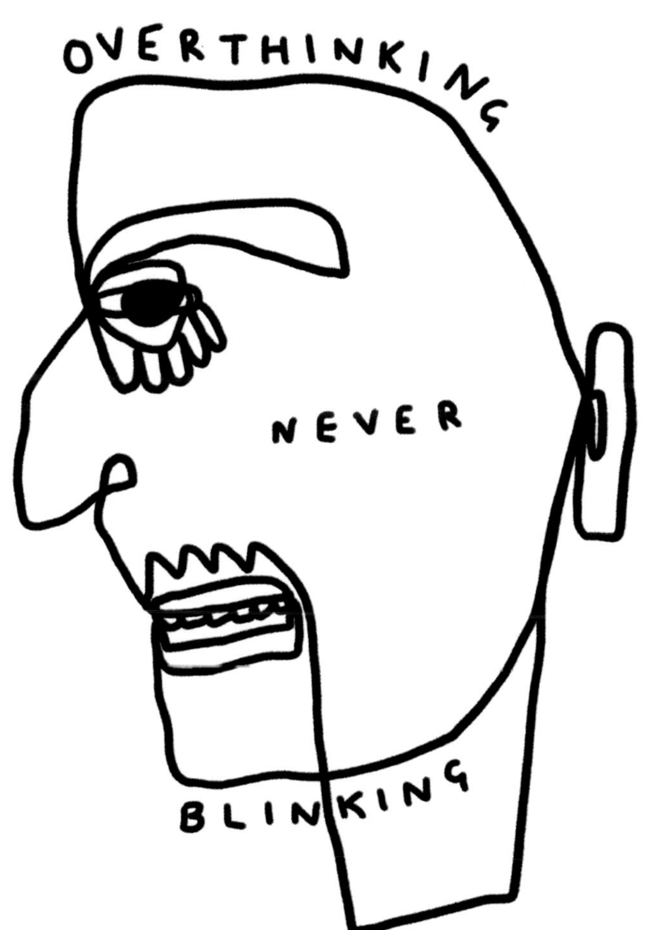
OVERTHINKING
NEVER
BLINKING

i hide under tables at parties

PEOPLE WITH ADHD HAVE MORE TOES

I AM NOT JOKING

having a great time
being alive

Clap clap clap! you made it through another day

I DIDNT WAKE UP ON THE WRONG SIDE OF THE BED. I WOKE UP ON THE DAMN FLOOR.

THERE IS A VERY TINY MAN
LIVING IN MY HEAD FOR FREE
AND HE IS EXTREMELY MEAN

i am not crying i am
actually hysterically laughing

I WISH I WAS
A WORM BECAUSE
I AM VERY OVERWHELMED

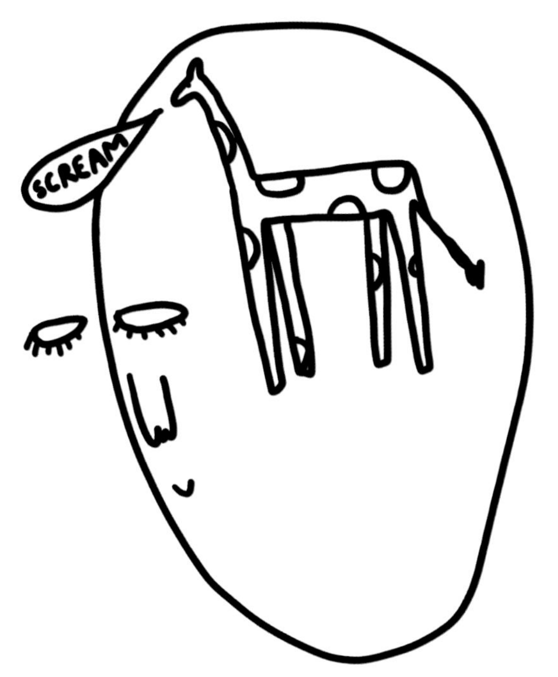

75th REASON WHY I CANT NAP

There is a giraffe in my head that screams whenever i close my eyes. His name is Simon.

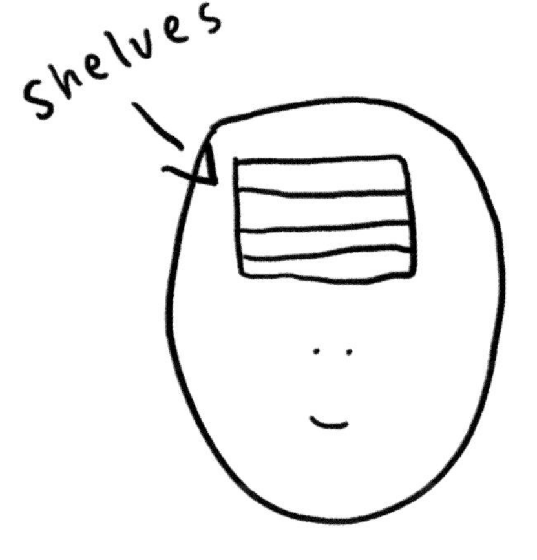

neurotypical
brain

neurodivergent
brain

PHILOSOPHY

everything
feels really
bad and then
it all feels
really good
and that is
just the way
it is

PEOPLE THINK I'M

JUST CONFUSED

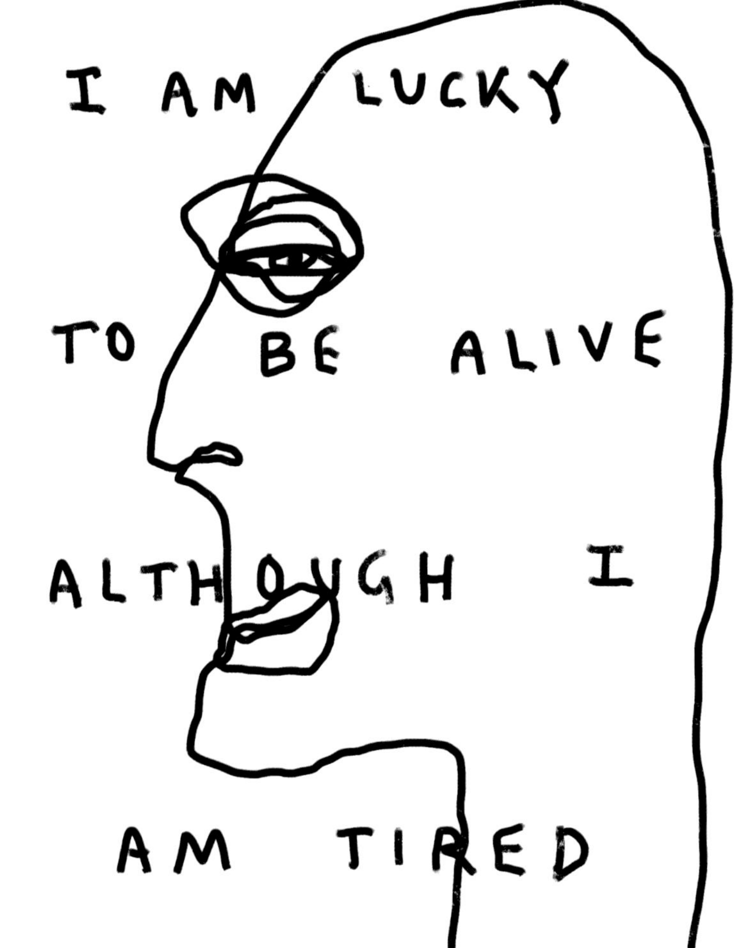
I AM LUCKY
TO BE ALIVE
ALTHOUGH I
AM TIRED

does anybody know why we

are on a floating ball in the middle of space thanks in advance

WHEN LIFE GIVES YOU LEMONS, JUST START SCREAMING

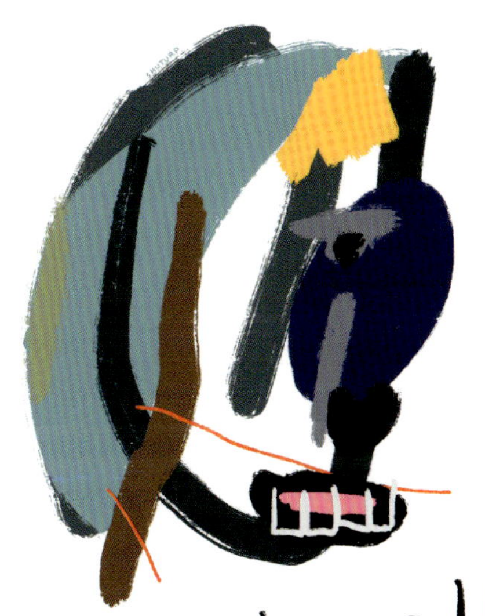

we're all on
the same ride just
different parts
like im going up slow
and you're coming down
fast.

running from problems

seems like a good idea

until it comes back with extra long hairy bits.

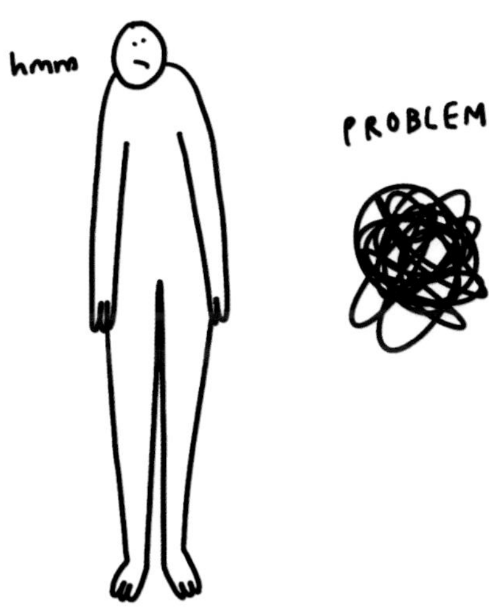

instead of running...

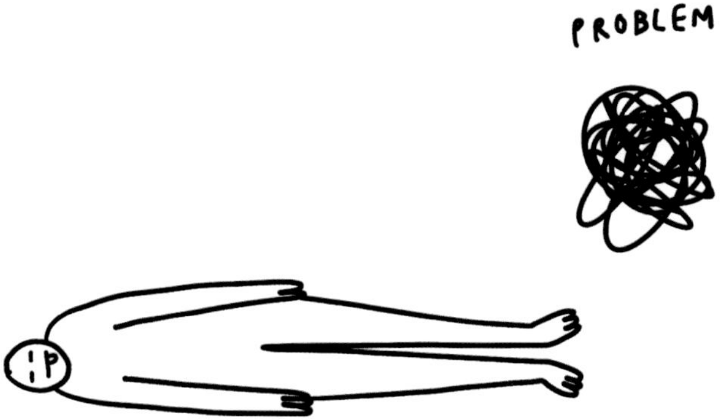

PROBLEM

pretend to be dead

everybody
has their
own shit

WHAT IS LIFE

AND WHY

I THINK YOU

MIGHT BE UPSET

AFTER YOU

REALISE THAT

YOU SPENT YOUR

WHOLE LIFE RUSHING.

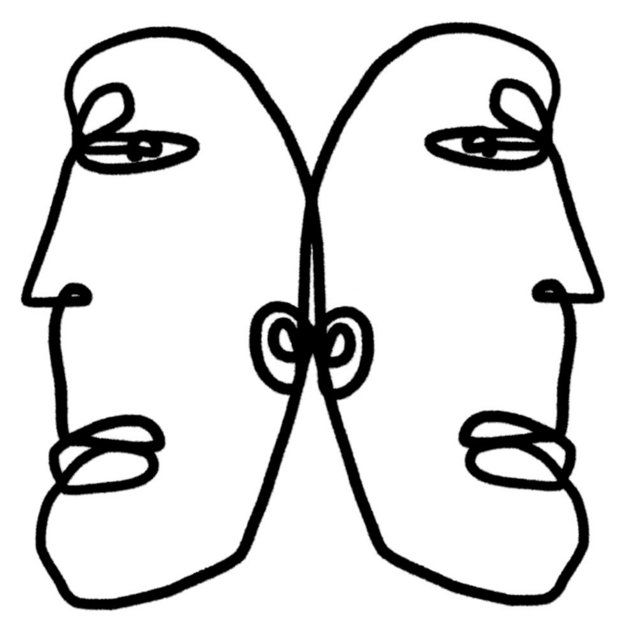

THINK GOOD
FEEL GOOD
POO GOOD

YOU CANT
PLEASE
EVERYONE

IF YOU KEEP
WAITING FOR THE
PERFECT TIME,
YOU'LL BE DEAD
WHEN IT ARRIVES

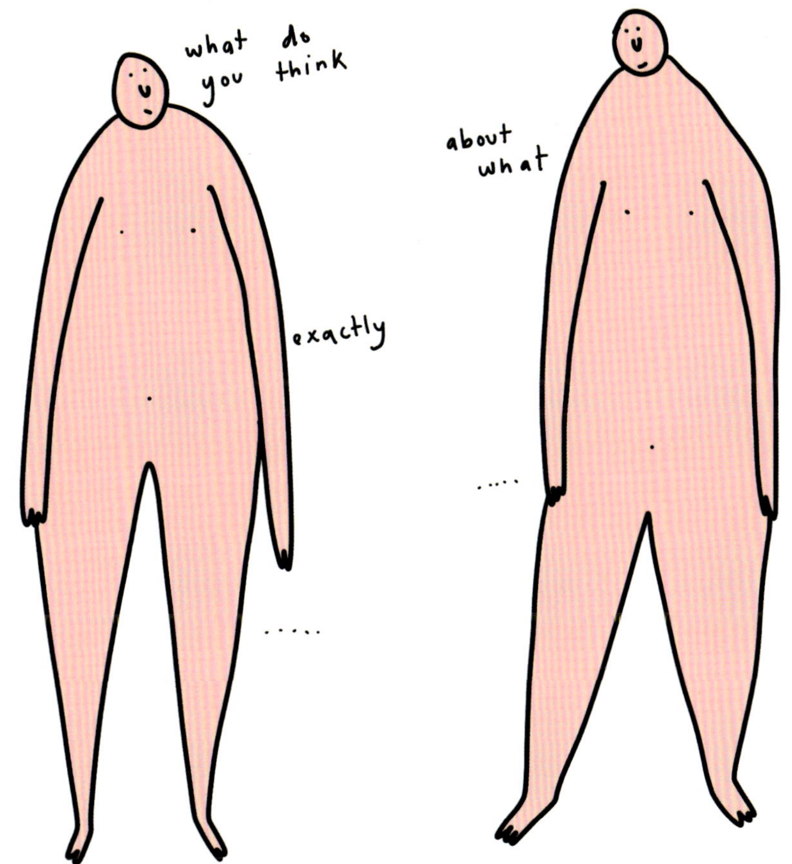
what do you think
about what
exactly
.....
.....

LICK Your ICECREAM
DO NOT BITE IT PLEASE

GIDDY UP
LIFE SUCKS

LIFE IS SILLY

AND IT'S FULL OF PAIN

YOU CAN LAUGH
TILL YOU CRY

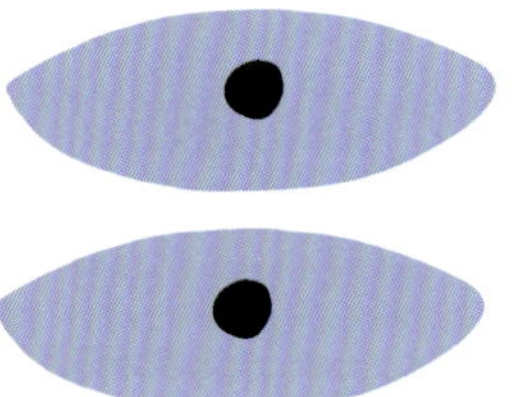

OR YOU CAN
POO IN THE RAIN

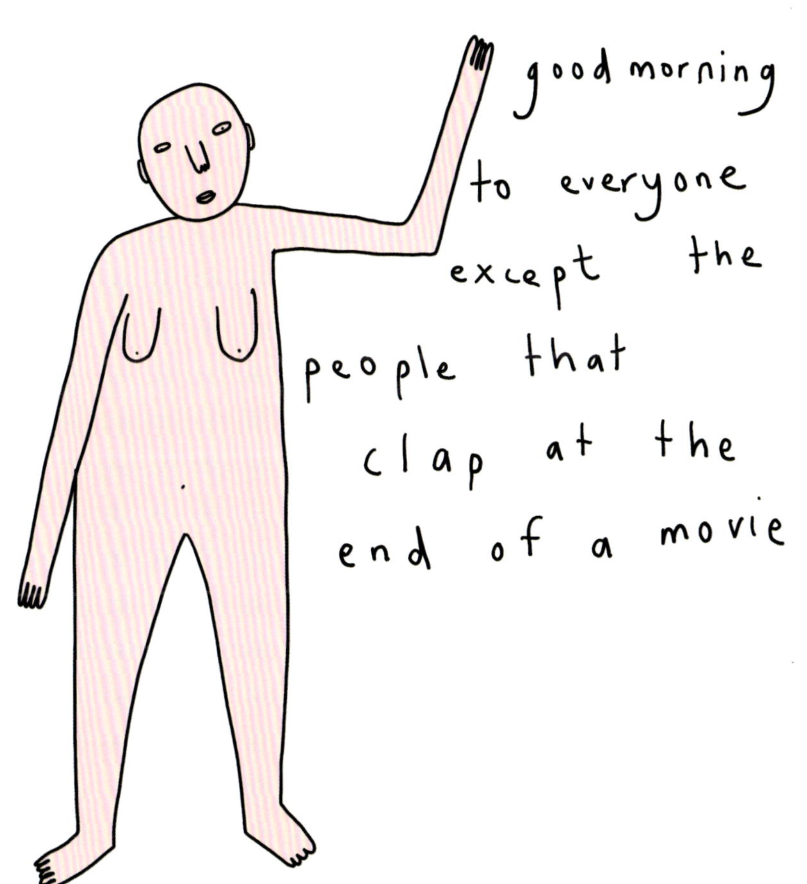
good morning
to everyone
except the
people that
clap at the
end of a movie

sometimes life
is really shit but
you just have to
get on with it

KEEP UR
HEAD UP

stay
calm
it's
fine

I ALWAYS HAVE ROOM FOR DESSERT

SELF-CARE

OUT OF ALL
THE THINGS
YOU COULD GIVE
DON'T GIVE
UP

YOUR BEST
IS ENOUGH

SLEEPING LIKE AN ANGEL
KNOWING FULL WELL THAT
I AM IN FACT NOT AN ANGEL

here is a lady laying
in some grass which
looks very relaxing

here is a flower if
you're feeling lonely

DO SOME YOGA

DO SOME PAINTING

EAT HEAPS

BUILD A FORT

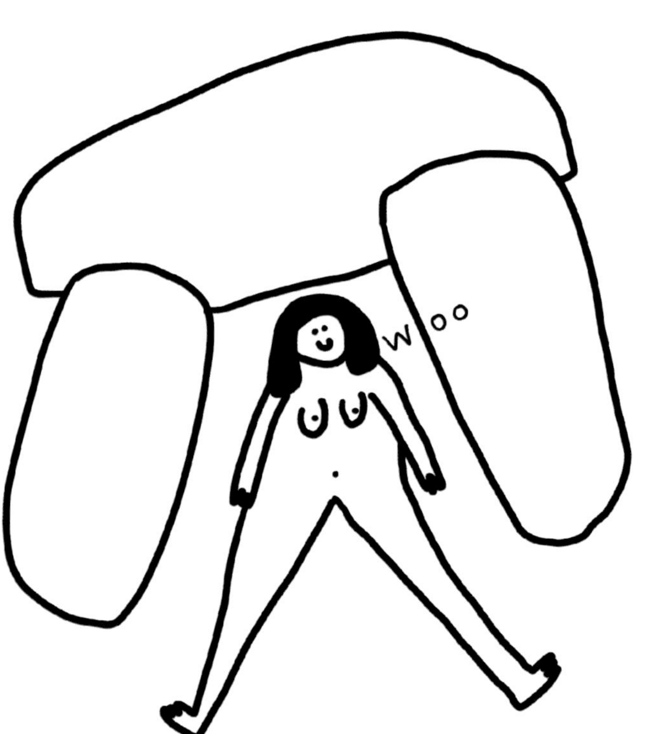

DO NOTHING

WHEN I AM HAVING A BAD DAY

I PUT MY HAPPY PANTS ON

AND THEN MY DAY IS STILL BAD

hahaha
don't

i need
a fucking
holiday

i love push-ups

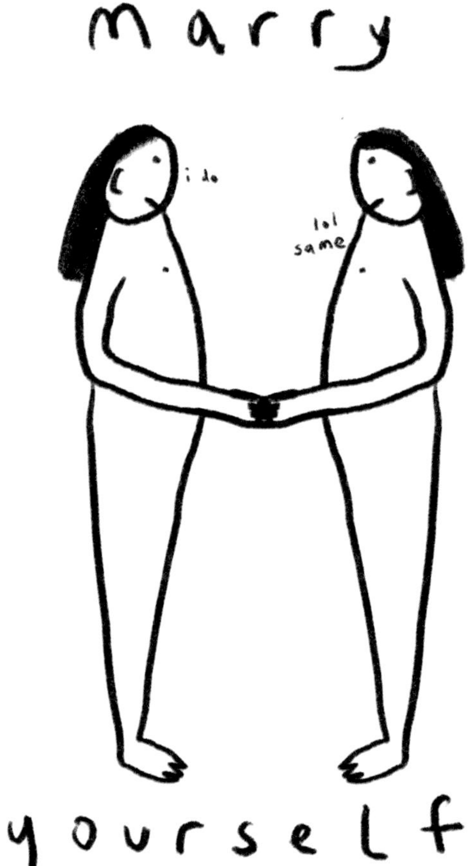

marry

i do

lol same

yourself

silly little walk
for my silly little head

SHIT'S FUCKED

GO NUTS

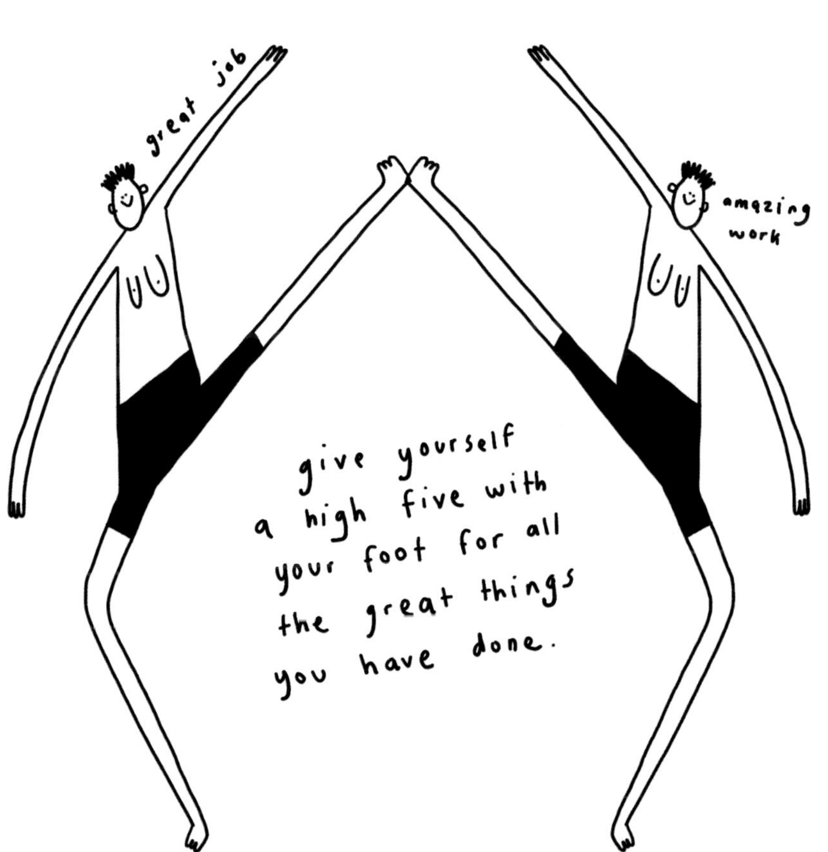
great job
amazing work
give yourself a high five with your foot for all the great things you have done.

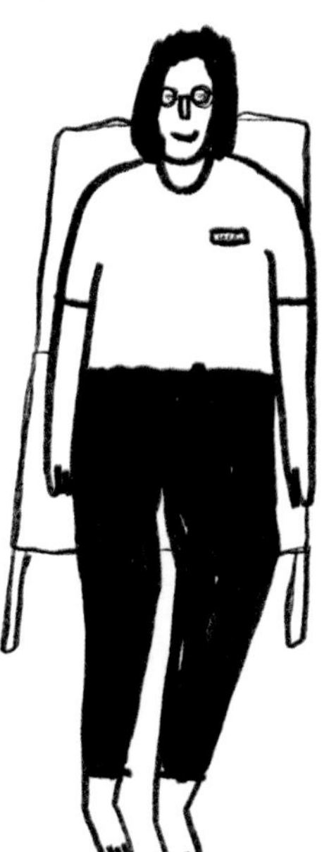
my name's sara and i'm an alcoholic

my name's mike and i have been playing candy crush for 43 days straight

MEDITATION

KEEP IN TOUCH WITH YOUR FAMILY

HUG
YOURSELF

try and laugh at
yourself in the mirror
while you are crying
every now and then

whoever said money
can't buy happiness
has obviously never
had chocolate pud.

i am
bad at
talking about
myself nicely.

sometimes you've
just gotta get
your nails and
lashes dun

the sun
makes me
feel good

baths are so boring don't act like they're not

sometimes you just need to lay down and look at the sky to remember how hot and dangerous you really are

DO NOT
TRY
SO
HARD

LET
IT
BE

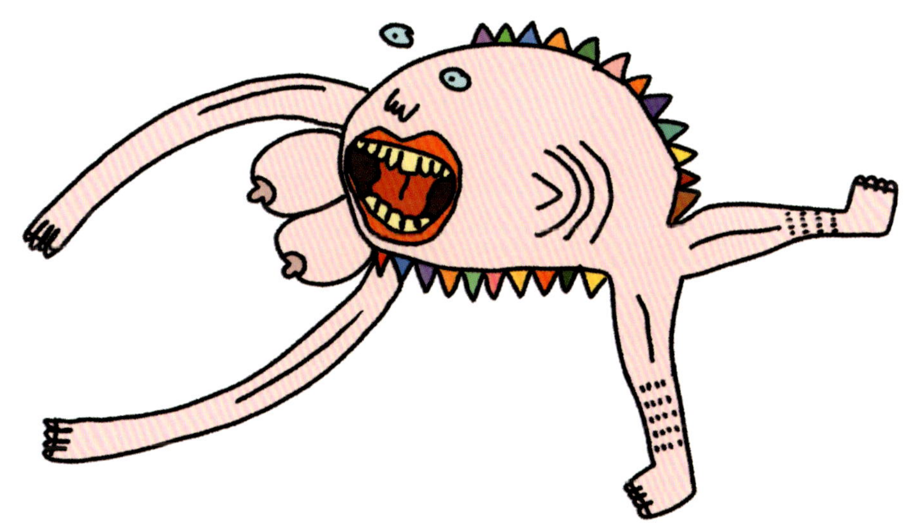

JUST KEEP SWIMMING UNTIL YOU DIE

don't shave if you
don't want to

AND THEN I WENT OUTSIDE
AND EVERYTHING WAS FINE

SOCIALISING
HELP

hi im sue
nice to meet you sue, i'm fucked

HOW TO
BE MEAN
LIKE EVERY-
ONE ELSE

be nice but not
so nice that people
think you're too
nice because sometimes
being too nice can
lead to things that
are not nice

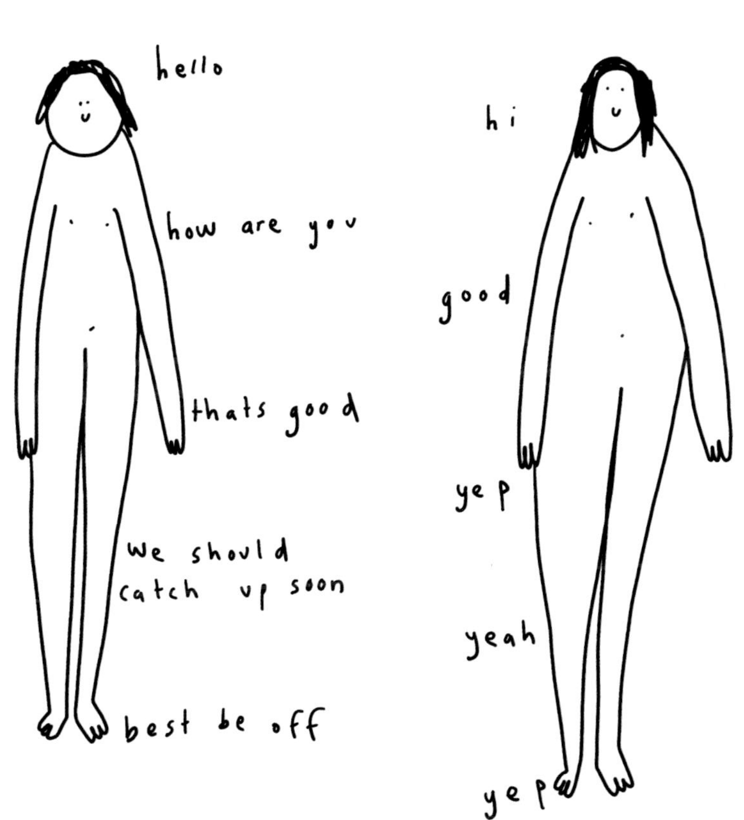
hello
hi
how are you
good
thats good
yep
we should
catch up soon
yeah
best be off
yep

hiya i was wondering if you wanted to come watch my band play on Friday night
Let me check my schedule

MY SCHEDULE

1 YOU	2 ARE	3 DOING	4 ABSOL
5 UTELY	6 FUCK	7 ING	8 NOTH
9 ING	10 YOU	11 BORING	12 SOD

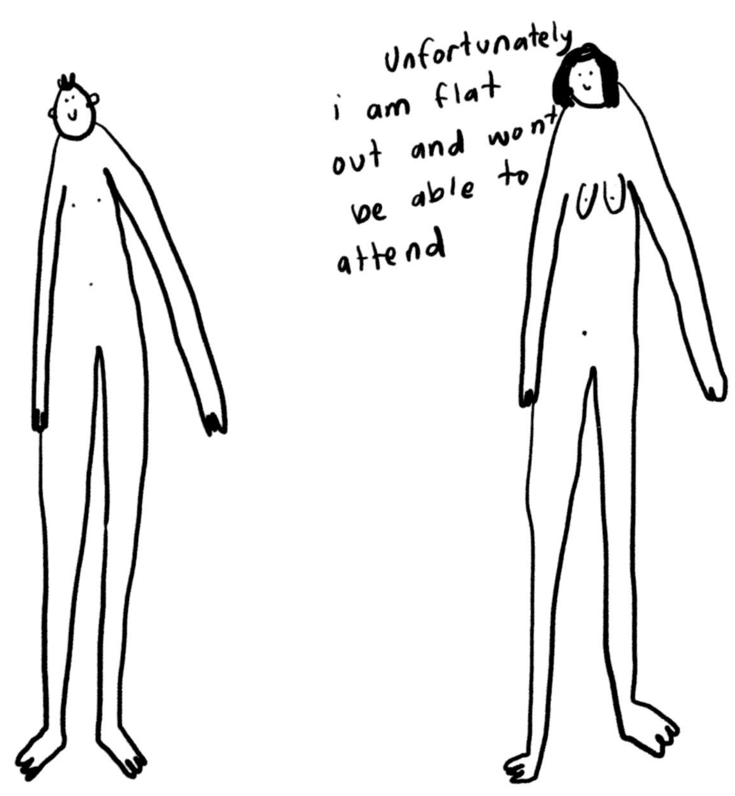
Unfortunately
i am flat
out and won't
be able to
attend

i'd love for the aliens
to come and get me

hi i would like to apply for a job
yes
this is a dog park

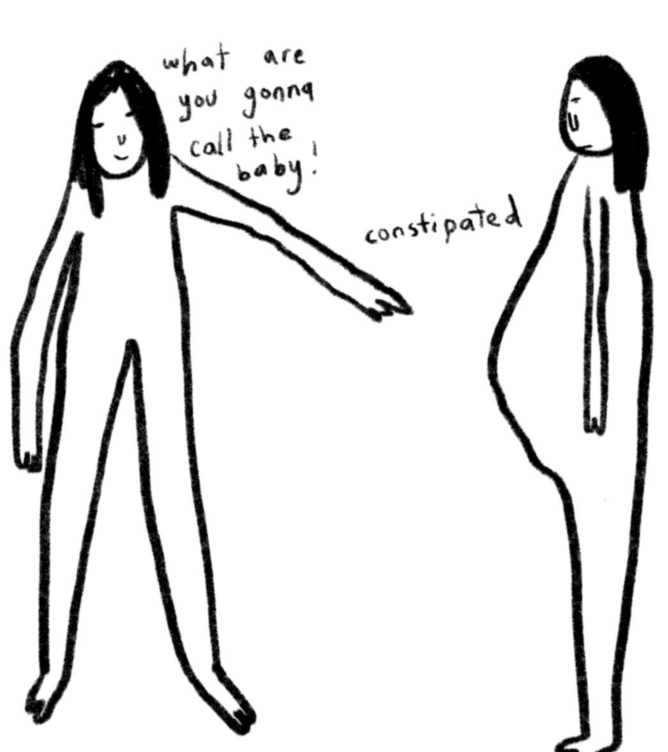
what are you gonna call the baby!
constipated

so are u
an introvert
or
what ?
oh no
i just
don't
like u

hey im
kevin
no
thanks

HELLO

GOOD
THANKS

i've got
a lot on my
plate and i'm
not that
hungry

WHY HAVEN'T YOU INVITED ME TO DINNER
BECAUSE YOU ALWAYS SAY NO
IT'S MAKING ME FEEL VERY SAD AND ALONE
OK SORRY WOULD YOU LIKE TO COME TO DINNER
NO SORRY

Hey im Pen!
Is that short for penny?
Oh no its just Pen. My mum loves pens. My brother is called post-it note.
oh

Body language is good when you dont feel like speaking

STAR SIGNS

ARIES

TAURUS

im gonna
need everyone to
shutup and let
me enjoy the
serenity thanks

GEMINI

CANCER

LEO

pay attention
to me immediately
i am not
joking cheers

VIRGO

LIBRA

the fact that my pants are rolled up unevenly is making me feel physically ill.

SCORPIO

SAGITTARIUS

I AM GOING ON A
VERY LARGE
WALK FOR
NO REASON
AT ALL

CAPRICORN

AQUARIUS

i want to do stuff but i also hate everyone so im in a slight pickle

PISCES

I AM FINE

everyone elses shit.

About the Author

Ellie Hopley (aka @shuturp) is a Gold Coast based artist who's been unapologetically herself since 1992. She lives a pretty quiet life with her dogs and close friends. Her favourite drink is vodka lemonade – or 100% pure orange juice delivered intravenously 24/7. Ellie does everything very quickly (a side effect of her ADHD), including drawing, walking and breathing. She would like everyone to keep up.

ACKNOWLEDGEMENTS

thank you to my parents for giving birth to such a funny hot person. this book would suck if i was boring. Shout out to my dogs for keeping me alive and lastly, the biggest thank you to YOU for supporting me and allowing me to do what i love every day. I love you!

First published by Affirm Press in 2023
Boon Wurrung Country
28 Thistlethwaite Street
South Melbourne VIC 3205
affirmpress.com.au

1 3 5 7 9 10 8 6 4 2

A catalogue record for this book is available from the National Library of Australia

ISBN: 9781922848352 (hardback)

Cover and internal design by Sasha Beekman © Affirm Press
Cover illustrations by Ellie Hopley © Shuturp
Printed and bound in China by C&C Offset Printing Co., Ltd.